Conrad K. Butler

THE BIGGEST TRUCKS IN THE WORLD

for kids

BELAZ 75710

BELAZ 75710 CAN BE CALLED A DUMPER, BUT NOT NECESSARILY A TRUCK. THIS IS BECAUSE IT CAN NOT BE DRIVEN ON PUBLIC ROADS. IF IT NEEDS TO BE TRANSPORTED, 25 RAILCARS ARE NEEDED!

BELAZ 75710
75710
450 Tons
BELAZ

450
BELAZ
7555H
BELAZ

CATERPILLAR 797B

CATERPILLAR
CATERPILLAR
797
109
104

CATERPILLAR
CAT
CAT
C3

THE LIEBHERR T 284 MINING TRUCK

THE LIEBHERR T284 MINING DUMP TRUCK IS THE LIGHTEST (LOWEST CURB WEIGHT) AND MOST EFFICIENT (HIGHEST PAYLOAD) ULTRA-CLASS MINING TRUCK, OFFERING AT THE SAME TIME LOWER FUEL CONSUMPTION AND A POWER OF OVER 4,000 HP. THIS IMPROVED MACHINE ENABLES CUSTOMERS TO MEET PRODUCTION TARGETS WITH FEWER TRUCKS OR IN LESS TIME.

LIEBHERR
284

DTU 003
DTU 002
DTU
FIRST QUANTUM
LIEBHERR
284
003

TEREX/BUCYRUS MT6300AC DUMP TRUCK

THE BUCYRUS MT6300AC IS AN OFF-HIGHWAY, ULTRA CLASS, TWO-AXLE, DIESEL/AC ELECTRIC POWERTRAIN HAUL TRUCK DESIGNED AND MANUFACTURED BY BUCYRUS INTERNATIONAL INC. IN THE UNITED STATES. THE MT6300AC IS BUCYRUS' LARGEST, HIGHEST PAYLOAD CAPACITY HAUL TRUCK, OFFERING ONE OF THE LARGEST HAUL TRUCK PAYLOAD CAPACITIES IN THE WORLD, UP TO 400 SHORT TONS (363 T).

DT017
TEREX/UNIT RIG
MT 6300AC
CITIC PACIFIC MINING
DT
NO UNAUTHORISED PARKING WITHIN 50 METRES
NO UNAUTHORISED PARKING WITHIN 50 METRES

T 282B
LIEBHERR

AUSTRALIAN ROAD TRAINS

THESE TRAINS ARE HUGE LONG TRUCKS, CONSISTING OF MANY TRAILERS. AUSTRALIAN ROAD TRAINS ARE A FASCINATING SETUP. THIS IS A BEHEMOTH, HUGE TRUCKS, AND TRAILERS THAT TRANSPORT CARGO IN THE WILD AUSTRALIAN OUTBACK.

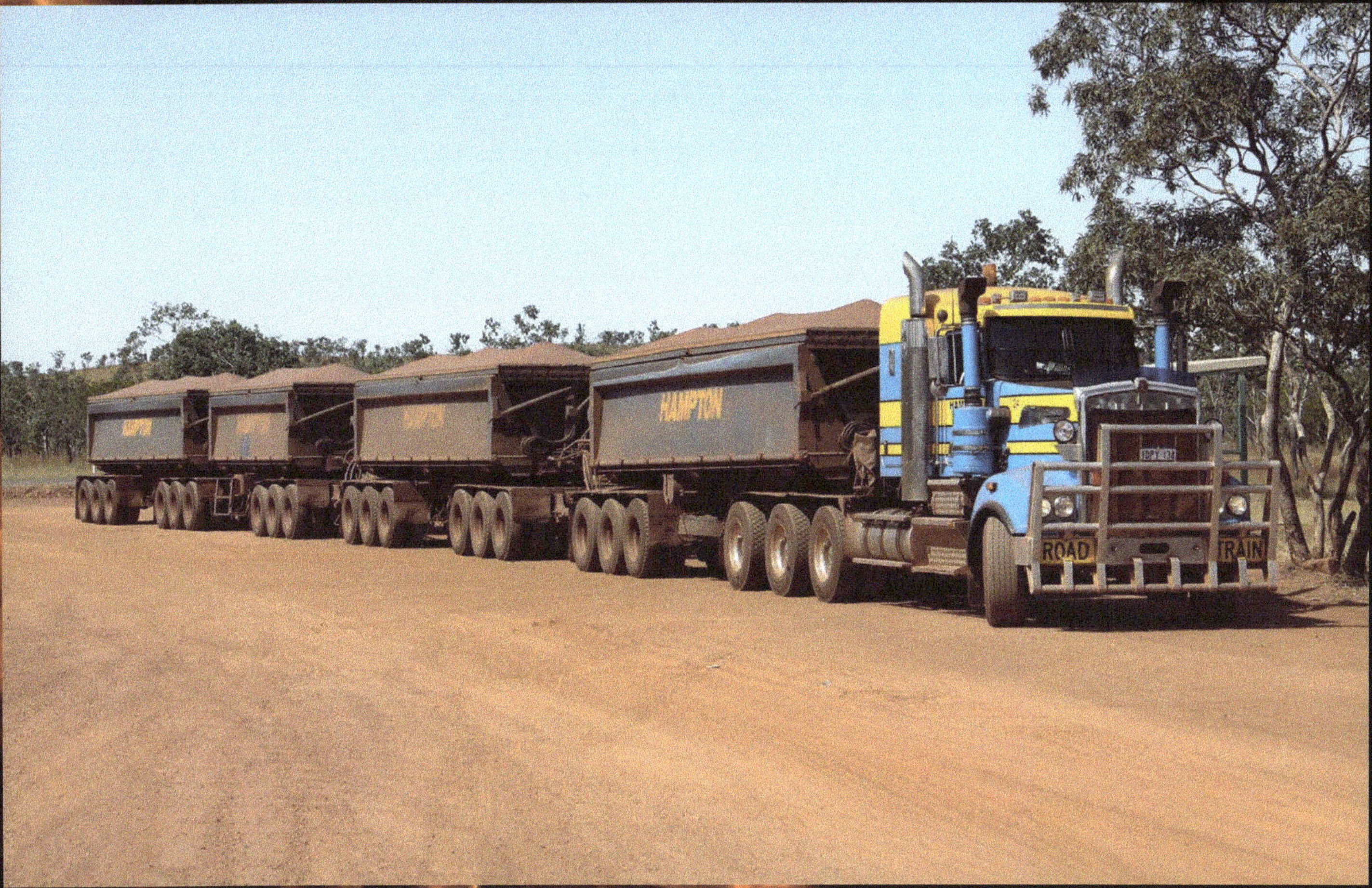
HAMPTON
ROAD
TRAIN

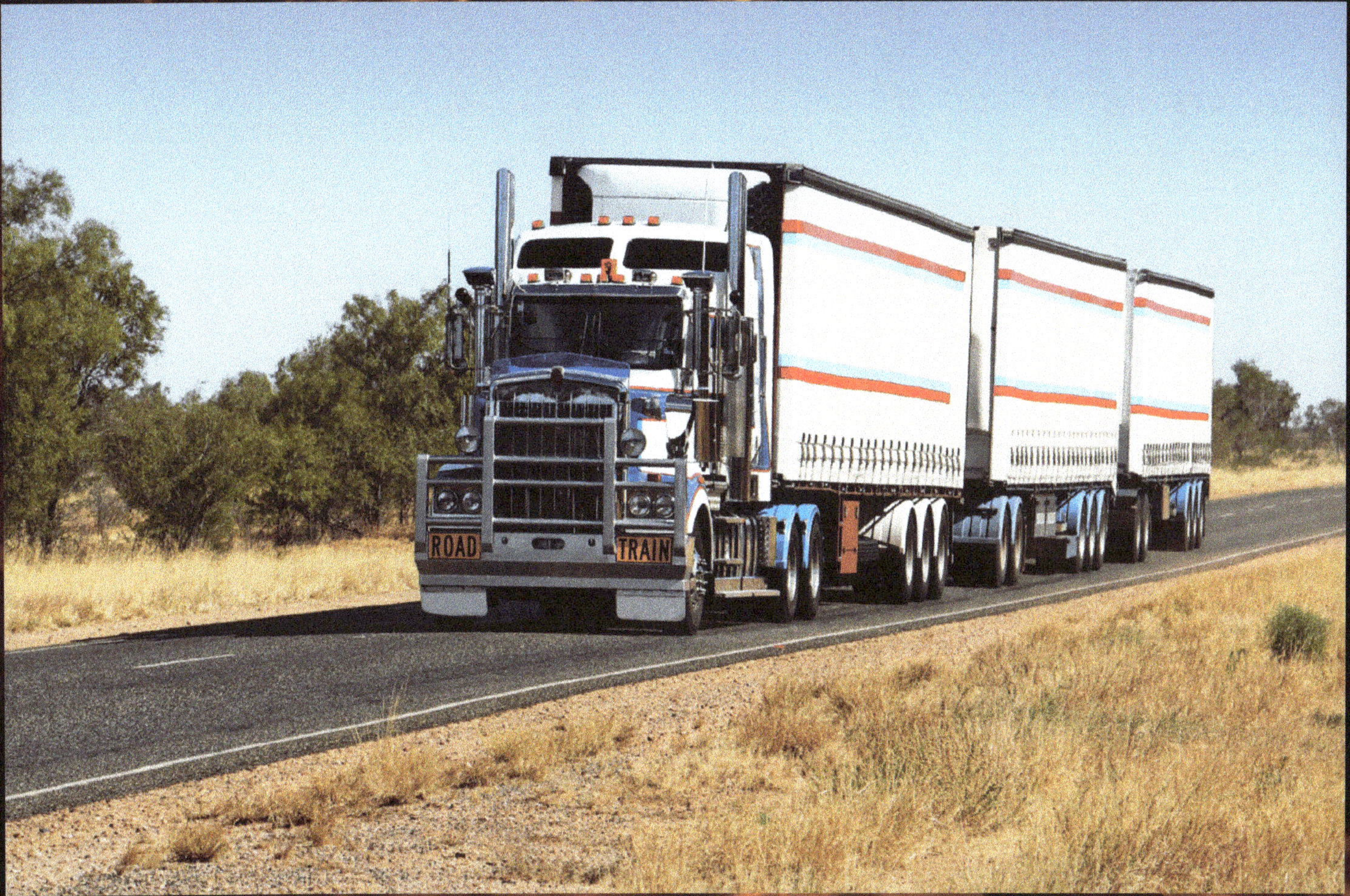
ROAD
TRAIN

KOMATSU 930E

THE 930E IS THE BEST-SELLING ULTRA CLASS HAUL TRUCK IN THE WORLD. AS OF SEPTEMBER 2016, KOMATSU HAS SOLD 1,900 UNITS OF 930E. [3][4] THE CURRENT MODEL, THE 930E-5 OFFERS A PAYLOAD CAPACITY OF UP TO 320 SHORT TONS (290 T).

930E

53

KOMATSU 930E
こまつの杜
2018 年 10 月 27日

BIGFOOT 5

BIGFOOT 5 IS A FORD MONSTER TRUCK FROM ST. LOUIS, MISSOURI, BUILT-IN 1986 AS THE TALLEST MONSTER TRUCK IN THE WORLD. THE TRUCK IS MOUNTED ON 10-METER TIRES. IN ADDITION TO ITS HEIGHT, BIGFOOT 5 IS ALSO THE HEAVIEST TRUCK EVER BUILT, WEIGHING 28,000 POUNDS.

XCMG DE400

THE LOAD CAPACITY OF THE VEHICLE REACHES 400 TONS, AND THE HIGHEST SPEED IS 30 MPH WITH A LIFTING TIME OF 24 SECONDS. THE VEHICLE CAN BE USED TO TRANSPORT MINES, METALS, STEEL, AND ALL MINERAL PRODUCTS IN THE OPEN AIR TO HELP INCREASE THE EFFICIENCY OF YOUR OUTDOOR MINING ACTIVITY AND LOWER THE AVERAGE COST.

TEREX 33-19 TITAN

SPARWOOD

SPARWOOD B.C.
TITAN

MERCEDES ZETROS

IF THERE IS A MERCEDES ZETROS IN THE AREA, KNOW THAT SOMETHING SERIOUS IS GOING ON. ESPECIALLY WHEN THE TOP MODEL ZETROS 3643 ENTERS THE GAME. IT IS A MACHINE THAT WILL ENTER WHERE OTHERS WOULD HAVE DIED LONG AGO.

ZETROS
1833
GER·XJ 104
MEILLER KIPPER

SELF-DRIVING
2733

VOLVO VNL 860

THE VOLVO VNL IS DESIGNED TO MEET THE NEEDS OF MODERN - AND FUTURE - LONG-HAUL HAULAGE. VNL OFFERS LONG-HAUL PERFORMANCE AS WELL AS PREMIUM COMFORT AND EQUIPMENT.

INKAS HURON

THE INKAS HURON TACTICAL ARMORED VEHICLE, A WELL-EQUIPPED ARMORED VEHICLE FOR BOTH MILITARY AND POST-APOCALYPTIC SURVIVAL OPERATIONS, FEATURES A BALLISTIC DESIGN WITH SPECIAL ARMOR PROTECTION. ADDITIONAL FEATURES INCLUDE AN EXPLOSION-PROOF FLOOR THAT IS IMPERMEABLE TO HAND GRENADES AND LAND MINES.

INKAS

DUNKEL INDUSTRIES LUXURY FORD F650 4X4

SIX PEOPLE CAN SLEEP IN IT AND TEN PEOPLE TRAVEL - THIS IS A VEHICLE THAT IS NOT A CLASSIC MOTORHOME, BUT SOMETHING THAT CAN BE CALLED A LUXURY CARAVANNING TRUCK. THIS IS WHAT THE FORD F-650 DUNKEL LUXURY HAULER 4X4 IS LIKE.

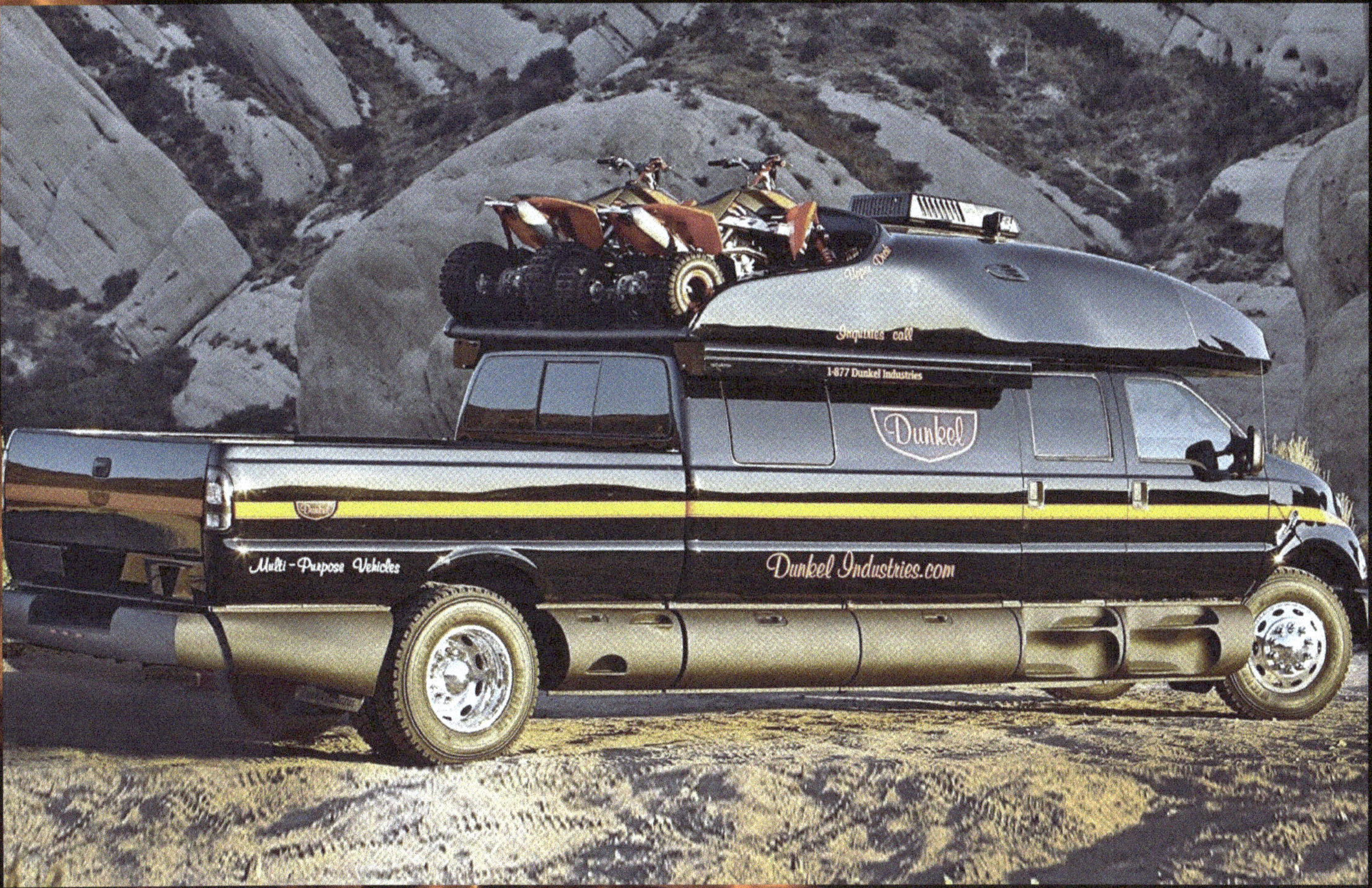
Inquiries call
1-877 Dunkel Industries
Dunkel
Multi-Purpose Vehicles
Dunkel Industries.com

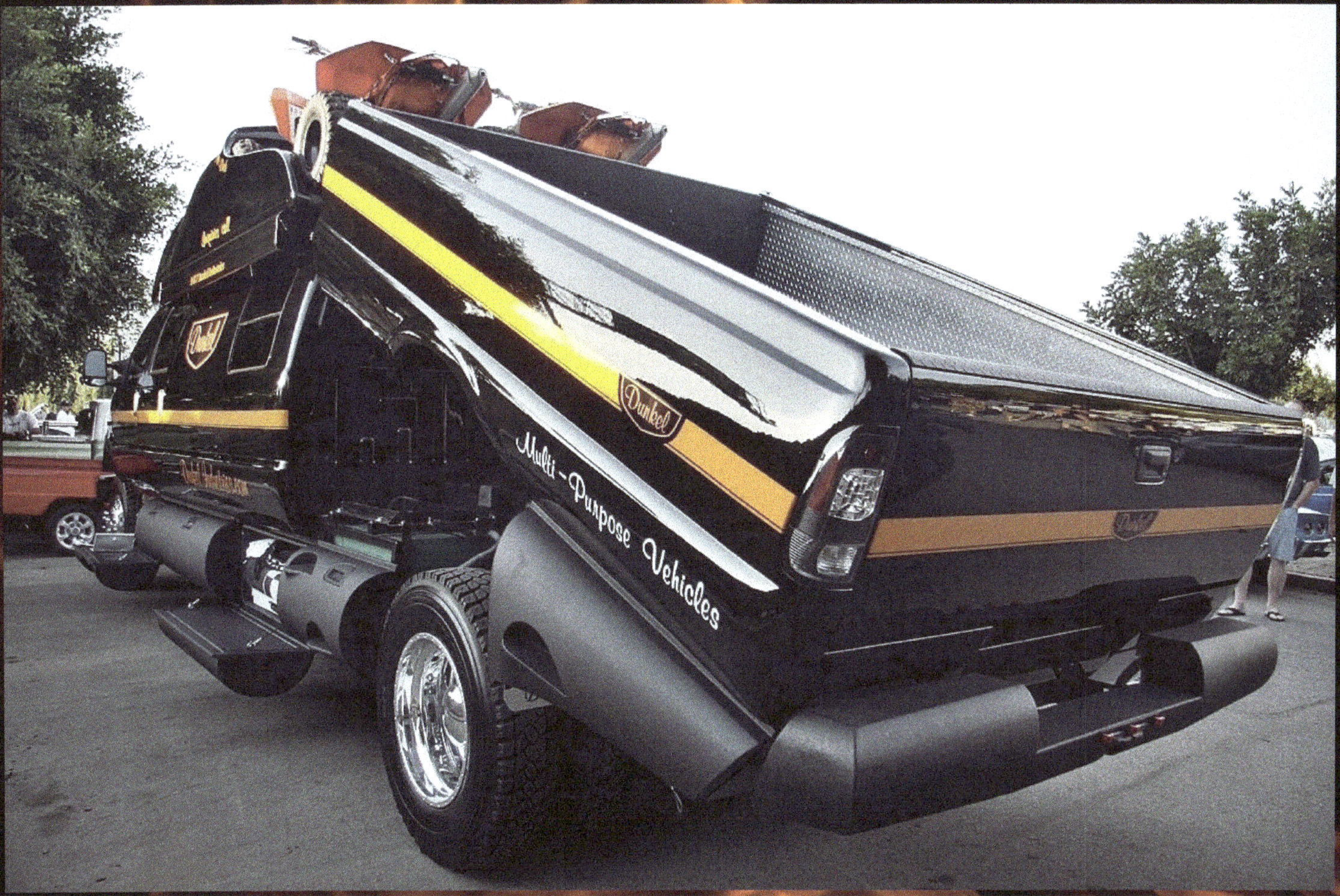
Dunkel
Multi-Purpose Vehicles

1950 DODGE POWER WAGON

THIS GIANT PICKUP TRUCK, MODIFIED FROM THE 1950'S MODEL, WAS THE BIGGEST PICKUP TRUCK EVER MADE. IT HOLDS FOUR AIR-CONDITIONED BEDROOMS, A LIVING ROOM, AND A BATHROOM, WITH A MOTORIZED TAILGATE THAT DROPS DOWN TO BECOME A TERRACE. THIS MONSTROSITY WAS COMMISSIONED BY BILLIONAIRE SHEIKH HAMAD IN THE UAE.

TRACTOMAS TR 10X10 D100

THE BIGGEST TRACTOR IN THE WORLD OF NICOLAS TRACTOMAS TR IS OPERATED IN SOUTH AFRICA SINCE 2005 WITH THE ADVENT OF THIS CAR, ALL THE FORMER ACHIEVEMENTS CONCERNED WITH THE WEIGHT OF THE TRANSPORTED CARGO WENT TO THE SHADOW, AND THE TRACTOR HIMSELF WAS DESERVEDLY PRESCRIBED IN THE GUINNESS BOOK OF RECORDS.

Eskom
Rotek Industries
NICOLAS
ABNORMAL/E
TRACTOMAS

TM01
TRACTOMAS

Check also:

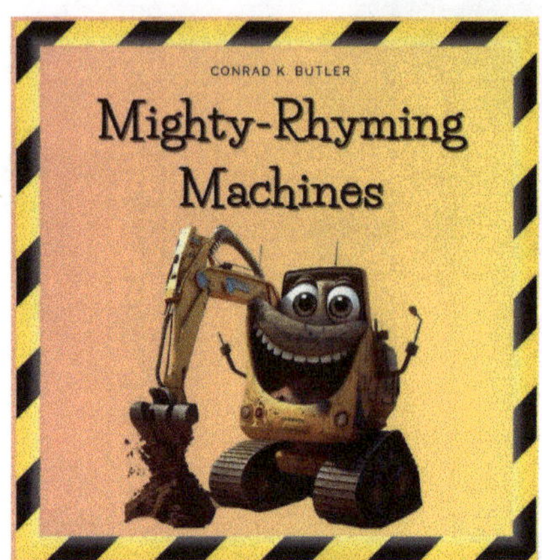

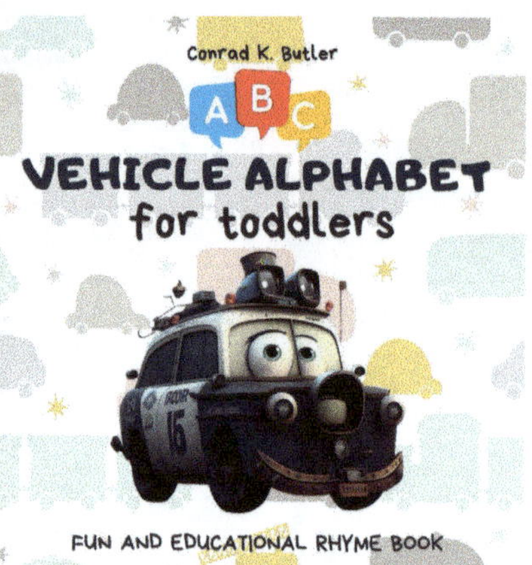

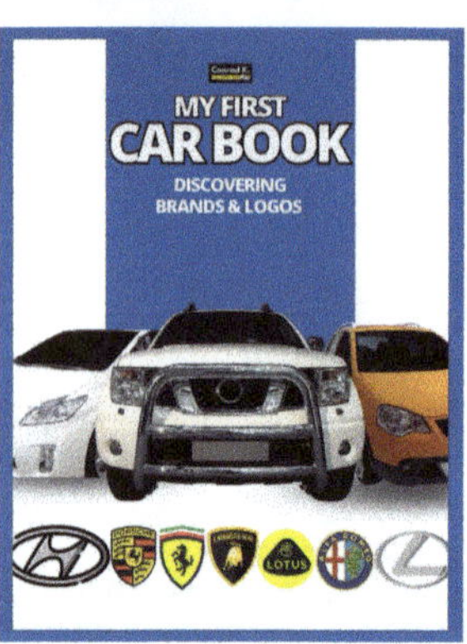

and much more!